# 365 Senior Moments
## You'd Rather Forget

Karen O'Connor

**HARVEST HOUSE PUBLISHERS**
EUGENE, OREGON

*Cover illustrations © gbreal / Fotolia; iStockphoto / touring*

*Cover design by Dugan Design Group, Bloomington, Minnesota.*

Published in association with the Books & Such Literary Agency, 52 Mission Circle, Suite 122, PMB 170, Santa Rosa, CA 95409-5370, www.booksandsuch.biz.

**365 SENIOR MOMENTS YOU'D RATHER FORGET**

Published by Harvest House Publishers
Eugene, Oregon 97402
www.harvesthousepublishers.com

ISBN 978-0-7369-4838-8 (pbk.)
ISBN 978-0-7369-4839-5 (eBook)

**Printed in the United States of America**

12 13 14 15 16 17 18 19 20 / BP-CD / 10 9 8 7 6 5 4 3 2 1

# The Chuckles Keep on Coming

Thank you to everyone who responded to my book *365 Reasons Why Gettin' Old Ain't So Bad*. I'm so glad you enjoyed it...and related to it. It's good to know I'm not alone! In *this* book you'll find 365 senior moments to steer clear of—if you can!

I hope these "senior moments," that seem to occur anytime and anywhere, will bring a smile of recognition, a playful warning, and a funny bone tingling when it comes to the absentminded and sometimes embarrassing things we do as we come down the other side of the mountain. I had fun putting them together based on my own missteps, those of friends and family, and even strangers who shared some of their "Oops!" moments with me.

If you'd like to add your own gaffes to my growing collection, please feel free to send them to me at karen@karenoconnor.com. I look forward to hearing from you!

Karen O'Connor
Watsonville, California

Parking your car on the east side of the mall, walking out the west side, and then panicking when you can't find your vehicle. That's not so bad. It's when you report it stolen…

Mistaking chocolate syrup for barbecue sauce when preparing pork ribs.

Spritzing your hair with furniture polish instead of hairspray, although both leave a nice sheen.

Turning the bathroom sink faucet on and then leaving to do something while it warms up, only to return to a flood.

Brushing your teeth with antifungal foot cream that's in a tube similar to your toothpaste.

Going down the slide at the playground with your grandchild and landing hard on your new hip.

Using a cup of salt instead of a cup of sugar in a cake recipe.

Putting your symphony tickets in a safe place and then forgetting where they are when you need them.

Agreeing to meet a friend at Tenth and Central on May eighth and then showing up at Eighth and Central on May tenth.

Planting bulbs you thought were tulips in the fall and being surprised when daffodils pop up in the spring.

Arriving at your water aerobics class and realizing you forgot to pack your swimming suit.

Putting your motel keycard to room 311 in the slot for room 211 and then raising a ruckus with the manager when the door won't open.

Trying to read a book and then realizing you have your spouse's glasses on.

Buying a shirt you like, only to get home and find an identical one in your closet.

Signing up for a class and then realizing when you arrive that you've already taken it.

Placing your umbrella on top of your car, driving off, and wondering later why it isn't in the car since you distinctly remember picking it up.

Trying to get cash from an ATM machine using a department store credit card.

Slipping into shoes of the same style without looking and then later having a friend point out that one shoe is blue and one is brown.

Taking photos with a disposable camera and then tossing the camera before developing the film.

Adding in your checkbook register when you should have subtracted.

Going outside to take your dog for a stroll and then realizing you brought the leash but forgot to grab Fido.

Placing a new kitchen sponge in the toaster instead of a slice of bread.

Laundering your money by leaving your wallet in your pants on washday.

"Storing" your glasses on top of your head and then asking someone to help you find them.

Putting an envelope in the mailbox without addressing it first.

Standing up so quickly that the muscles in your legs and feet haven't had time to wake up and cooperate. Then you're embarrassed by the fuss because everyone rushes over to help and asks if you're all right.

Running out to your car when you hear an alarm sounding and then realizing your car doesn't have an alarm.

Writing a reminder note and then forgetting to read it.

Putting a pan of water on to boil, doing
something else while you wait, and
returning to find the pot empty, char-
coal black, and bonded to the burner.

Borrowing a book from the library, forgetting to act on the notices to return
it, and finding out a year later the fine
you owe is more than the book is worth.

Putting your kitchen towels in the trash compactor instead of a drawer.

Selecting a hairstyle you like from a magazine photo, making an appointment with a stylist, and then forgetting to take the picture with you.

Jumping several times to grab the rope on the garage door to close it, not realizing that what your daughter always refers to as the "garage door opener" also shuts it.

Calling a friend to share the latest news in the neighborhood and then drawing a blank—forgetting the news, the names of the people involved, and why your friend would be interested.

Waiting until nightfall to appreciate how lovely the day was instead of really enjoying it at the time.

Purchasing a book to improve your memory and then leaving it at the checkout counter.

Dropping your socks and shirt in the gardening basket and your garden tools in the laundry hamper.

Rummaging in your purse for your cell phone, only to realize it's already clipped on your ear.

Using suntanning lotion when you meant to apply sunscreen.

Dabbing your wrists with insect repellant instead of cologne.

Making a lunch date with a friend for Mexican food and then being upset when one of you shows up at El Pollo Loco and the other at El Torito.

Jumping out of bed at nine o'clock and realizing you've overslept for a morning appointment. You rush like crazy and then, upon arrival, discover you're actually 24 hours early.

After opening the mail, instead of shredding the envelope, you shred the letter.

Dropping the boat anchor at your favorite fishing spot and then realizing you forgot to tie it to the boat.

Phoning a friend and forgetting who you called when someone answers the phone.

Returning to the store about a missing item you know you paid for...only to find it later already put away on a shelf in the pantry.

Trying to pay your utility bill at the hardware store and being indignant when the clerk doesn't understand.

Putting a quick meal into the microwave, cutting up a piece of fruit, and toasting a slice of bread and cheese for a delightful lunch—and then finding a shriveled meal in the microwave the next morning.

Taking your car in to resolve a sloshing sound and paying big bucks to learn that a bottle of water had fallen under the driver's seat.

Getting ready to set up a tent at your campsite and realizing your grandkids forgot to repack the poles when they borrowed it.

Placing a bag of groceries next to the car while you unlock the door and then wondering what happened to the groceries when you arrive home without them.

Answering the phone by putting the TV remote to your ear.

Putting your car keys in your jacket pocket so you won't lose them and then searching everywhere but there when it's time to go.

Cutting your own hair to save money and being shocked at the result.

Setting out pills for your pet next to your own and then taking the pet pills yourself and giving yours to the cat.

Pushing a full grocery cart out to your car, unloading the groceries into the trunk, and then leaving your purse in the cart when you drive off.

Inviting a friend to an event and getting upset when she doesn't show, only to find out later you gave her the wrong date.

Going out the front door, returning to pick up your jacket, going out again and locking the door, only to realize you left your keys on the counter when you stopped to put your coat on.

Scolding your mate about misplacing his Bible and then discovering you can't find your own when you meet for Bible study.

Hiding a piece of chocolate from a family member on a diet, only to find it melted in your purse or pocket the next day.

Buying a birthday gift for a loved one and then discovering you gave the *same* treasure to the *same* person the year before.

Reaching for the shaving cream and ending up with foaming hand soap all over your face because you hadn't yet put on your glasses.

Inviting a group for lunch on May 4 but circling May 14 on your calendar.

Opening your mailbox at the post office and leaving the key in the lock when you go back to your car.

Swigging a tall glass of chicken broth when you thought you'd grabbed the lemonade.

Dashing out the door to shop and then nearly dropping with embarrassment when someone points out that the hem of your nightgown is hanging below the hem of your dress.

Going to a meeting at work and not discovering you put your shirt on inside out until lunch time.

Leaving your house key in the front door and then going to sleep feeling totally secure.

Searching for your favorite pen and finding it perched behind your ear.

Putting a gallon of ice cream in the refrigerator instead of the freezer. (And being thankful your roommate discovered it and graciously cleaned up the mess.)

Offering to teach a class on memory enhancement and then forgetting to show up for the first session.

Introducing your aging parents to a group of friends as Mom and Dad because you can't recall their given names.

Cutting a recipe meant for six down to two when you're serving dinner for four because you're not a math whiz.

Promising your friend tickets you can't use for a play and then forgetting to pass them on until the day after the event is over.

Hanging out with people who say you look good for your age…and then wondering if they mean you look good or you look your age.

Running all over the house looking for your tennis shoes and then remembering you left them in your locker at the gym.

Purchasing a new floor heater because the one you have doesn't work and then realizing it would have if you'd turned it on or plugged it in.

Storing your pots in the oven because your cupboard is full and then forgetting to take them out before preheating the oven for baking cookies.

Grabbing the furniture oil instead of the tanning oil when you're going outside on a sunny day.

Tossing your dirty clothes down the trash chute instead of the laundry chute.

Changing the wrong tire on your car after someone pointed out one is going flat.

Spending almost an hour getting a photo matted and placed in the frame just right and then realizing when you flip it over that the photo is upside down.

Heating a cup of coffee in the microwave while you do a quick errand and then forgetting about it...but wondering the rest of the day what happened to your favorite mug.

Paying an auto technician to find the source of an annoying clicking sound, only to be told the culprit is your grandchild's box of miniature cars lost among the emergency supplies stowed in the trunk.

Trying to turn on the TV with your cell phone.

Carefully applying stamps to the upper right-hand corner of each Christmas card envelope and then noticing the envelopes were piled upside down so the stamps are now on the lower left-hand corners.

Leaving the tent at night to take care of business and not remembering that bears are around until you are alone and on your way back with only a flashlight for protection.

Ordering a new set of dentures because you misplaced the old ones...and then finding them in a drawer in the bathroom.

Speaking with enthusiasm in front of a group of people who appear distracted by something and discovering later your fly was open.

Patching an item with superglue while talking to someone and gluing yourself to it.

Driving to the grocery store in your husband's car and then reporting *your* car lost when you can't find it after shopping.

Setting your coffee cup on top of your car while you unlock the door and then watching in your rearview mirror as it bounces down the road when you take off.

Introducing your new spouse to a group of old friends and blanking out when it comes to his or her name, putting you in the doghouse before you reach your first anniversary.

Telling your mate you need a little time to think about something before you answer and then forgetting about it for a week.

Showing your grandkids photos of yourself as a child or teen and having to spend an hour convincing them that, yes, that's really you.

Waiting for your clothes to dry in a small-town Laundromat at the end of a vacation and then realizing after a while that you forgot to put coins in the slots.

Talking to yourself when no one is around and then looking up to discover your neighbor is looking at you strangely. Of course, if talking to yourself is the only way to get the answers you want to hear, it might be worth it.

Shaving your legs so you feel presentable but realizing later you forgot to pluck the hairs on your chin.

Putting mascara and eye shadow on one eye, answering the phone, and forgetting to go back and do the other one.

Rushing while in a public bathroom and discovering later you have a dangling tail of toilet paper tucked into your pants or pantyhose.

After taking a shower, liberally applying self-tanning mousse to your hair.

Joining a conversation by saying how
much you like Spam...only to discover
your friends were talking about junk
emails.

Purchasing a book you've always wanted
to read at a garage sale and discovering it's the fourth copy you've bought
this year.

Trying to light a burner on an electric stove with a match. (It might take more time than you have.)

Hitting a bug on your kitchen counter with a flyswatter and discovering after you put your glasses on that it was a stray blueberry.

Hunting for the nails you need for a carpentry project when they're hanging out of your mouth.

Putting a pot of fresh veggies on a stove burner and wondering why the food is cold 15 minutes later, and then remembering that burner hasn't worked for years.

Leaving home without your dentures.

Getting into an elevator and talking with your friends, finally noticing the elevator isn't moving because no one pressed the up button.

Putting your favorite sunhat in a safe place for the following summer and looking high and low for it…finally discovering it when you're searching for your mittens after the first snowfall.

Discovering your favorite pair of shoes lined up perfectly on a shelf in the bathroom instead of in the bedroom where they belong.

Hanging your glasses on a string around your neck and then hunting all over your house, yard, and car because you can't find them.

Ordering your fast-food lunch from a drive-through bank teller.

Sending a "congratulations on your new baby" to a senior citizen and a sympathy card to the mother of a newborn.

Trying to seal an envelope using lip balm instead of a glue stick.

Parking your car but forgetting to turn the engine off so that when you return it's out of gas.

Scolding your mate for misplacing his hearing aids and then discovering you can't find yours either.

Getting into a car with a stranger because you rushed out of the store and got into the vehicle you thought was your waiting son's. You've just reached destination embarrassment!

Phoning a friend for advice and then hanging up before she answers because you can't remember what you wanted to ask.

Rushing into a public restroom only to discover you've gone into the one for the opposite sex.

Shaking hands effusively with a person you've never met because you thought it was someone you knew.

Parking your car in the stadium lot before a baseball game and then not having any recollection of where you parked when the game is over.

Trying to return a purchased item of clothing at the customer service counter at the wrong store.

Using the word "autopsy" instead of "biopsy" when telling your friend you'll be praying for a good report.

Taking your grocery list into the voting booth and your voting list into the grocery store. Either way you'll be forced to rely on your memory, and you know where that can lead.

Enrolling in a night class marked "for seniors only" and finding out the intended audience is high school seniors.

Asking your hard-of-hearing mate to "pass the Jell-O" while watching TV and being surprised when he hands you a pillow.

Looking at photos of your wedding day and wondering what happened to the person you married.

Walking around with your bath towel wrapped around your body after a shower and suddenly realizing it fell off...somewhere.

Complaining that you feel like you're drowning when you wash your hair in the shower, only to be told that if you turn your back to the shower and then wash your hair you can avoid that problem.

Showing up for a wedding at church "A" when the invitation says church "B," and then rushing to the correct church realizing too late that you left your gift at the first church. The couple you've never met will sure be surprised!

Demanding a refund for a broken appliance because you have the original receipt, not realizing that after 20 years the warranty might be up.

Hopping into your neighbor's car that is the same model and color as yours and wondering why the stubborn motor won't kick over.

Asking for a senior discount in a store and then feeling miffed the clerk didn't ask you for your ID or, even worse, being given the senior discount without being asked for your ID!

Going to the doctor for pain in your feet only to realize you've been wearing a pair of new shoes that still has paper stuffed in the toes.

Adding sugar to a bowl of soup and salt to a cup of coffee.

Protecting your grandchildren's arms and backs with a tube of eye ointment instead of sunscreen.

Telling the same story over and over. If you catch yourself doing this, why not give it a new ending?

Lying down for a 15-minute nap that turns into 3 hours and then wondering why you're wide awake at two in the morning.

Relying on your memory for the recipe of a favorite dish you want to serve your children and grandchildren and then ending up taking everyone out for dinner because you forgot an essential ingredient...whatever it was.

Teaching your grandkids a card game you think you remember and then trying to be a good sport while they beat the socks off you.

Jumping on the trampoline with an active grandchild and then being surprised when you end up in Urgent Care.

Telling a joke and suddenly realizing you don't remember the punch line.

Giving verbal directions to someone with a memory just like yours...or worse.

Parking your car downtown without paying close attention to nearby landmarks so you have no idea where it is when you try to find it later.

Carefully making a shopping list...and then leaving it at home.

Signing up and paying for a cruise with friends and then remembering you get seasick.

Joining the church c̶
involved before recal̶
never done that before—̶
a tune.

Agreeing to make meals for shut-i̶
when your cooking skills run toward̶
hot dogs and opening cans of soup.

Volunteering to be on the disaster team
in your community when it takes
you an hour to get moving because
of arthritis.

...cusing your spouse of being irrespon-
...ble with the motel key card and sud-
...enly remembering you were the last
...ne to use it.

Inadvertently picking out the same
birthday card for your mate two years
in a row.

While on a trip by yourself absentmind-
edly getting in on the passenger side
of the car.

Saying to your spouse, "Tell the one about..." and then giving away the punch line.

Wearing two different earrings and then covering up by insisting you did it on purpose.

Trying to put in your contact lenses while leaning over the bathroom sink with the stopper open.

Cleaning your electric shaver on the balcony overlooking a flower bed with white blooms.

Turning on the hose to water the roses and then leaving for a week's vacation, coming home to a flooded front yard because you forgot to turn the water off.

Writing a check to the telephone company for the amount you owe the credit card company.

Carefully battening down your house before you leave on a trip but forgetting to close the garage door after you drive out.

Subjecting your spouse to an old movie on TV only to realize at the end that you've both already seen it.

Bragging about how well you keep house for someone your age until you double-check your progress by putting on your glasses.

Wiping your eyes with the hanky in your pocket and then tossing it, realizing too late that it was probably the 20-dollar bill you've been saving for a special purchase.

Pulling up to a mailbox on the corner, getting out to mail a letter and slamming the door, accidentally locking the car with the keys still in the ignition and the engine running.

Signing up for an adult education class without wearing your glasses and realizing you're now taking a geometry class instead of a gardening class.

Ordering a slice of sugar-free pie and washing it down with an ice-cream soda.

Laundering red shirts with white and wool socks with cotton and then complaining when you have to shop for a new wardrobe.

Saying yes to an invitation for a dinner date and then forgetting who asked you.

Refrigerating your car keys and putting the package of sliced ham into your purse after coming home from the store.

Using Easter seals on envelopes and mailing them and then wondering why you still have so many postage stamps.

Putting on your mate's reading glasses and then being perturbed when she can't find hers.

Falling behind the technology times by talking about birds when someone refers to tweeting.

Going ice-skating with grandchildren and then discovering it would have been a good idea to have a pair of crutches ready on the sidelines.

Teaching your grandkids never to speak to strangers and then being embarrassed when they won't say hello to a friend of yours they've never met.

Parking your car in your neighbor's driveway and then wondering where your car went.

Telling your grandkids God is watching over them and to trust Him for everything and then trying to figure out how to get them to look out for traffic when they ride their bikes on the street.

Being a backseat driver and then debating whether you should chip in for the traffic ticket the driver received for ostensibly following your advice.

Knitting a grandbaby sweater that, when completed, was a perfect fit for a seven-year-old.

Attending a class reunion and being surprised when no one recognized you as the handsome dude you once were.

Waking up in a hotel room panicked for a moment because you dreamed someone had kidnapped you.

Swatting at moving insects only to find they're really just floaters in your eyes.

Climbing up an extension ladder to put away a box of Christmas decorations on the top shelf and then realizing you left the box on the floor.

Following a long hike and setting up camp, you're ready to sit down to a well-deserved and longed for dinner...and realize you left the stove fuel in the car.

Calling your mate by your pet's name.

Writing a check for the groceries, grabbing your grocery bag and purse, and walking off—then being chased down by the clerk because you forgot to give him the check.

Holding your breath while praying and having to remind yourself that God asks you to pray without *ceasing*, not without *breathing*.

Feeling annoyed because of the route your spouse is taking to your destination, you start giving directions and suddenly discover you're not sure how to get there.

Standing in a long line to pay your property taxes, you discover when it's your turn that you left home without your checkbook or credit card.

Driving to the desert for a weekend campout you realize you forgot to fill up the water tank.

Seeing if you can blow bubbles with bubble gum-flavored ice cream.

Believing you can still do what you did when you were 24...and ending up in the emergency room.

Saying yes to attending a surprise birthday party for a friend and then being so excited you promptly call her to relate the exciting news.

Looking into a security camera in a store and using the reflection to put on your lipstick.

Confusing your age with your cholesterol count when someone asks you how old you are.

Waiting until the last minute to look for a public restroom, you're so desperate you consider resorting to one provided by nature—a large tree.

Spritzing your plants with hairspray.

Saying no to the carbs but yes to the fat.

Buying an item you don't need from the sale table because you're going to save five bucks.

Forgetting your best friend's name when introducing him or her to someone you just met.

Waking up from a late-afternoon nap and thinking it's morning, thereby starting your day at five o'clock.

Saying yes to an invitation to a party and then showing up on time but on the wrong day.

Arriving at work, you get out of your car and notice your special coffee cup with the nonslip bottom is still on the roof of your car where you'd put it when you unlocked the car door. No wonder so many people were waving at you on your way to work!

Wearing your nametag upside down all evening at a reunion or seminar. When you notice, you realize people probably thought you were confused or trying to be cute.

Rolling on Biofreeze pain medication instead of deodorant.

Putting dishwashing liquid in the fridge and pouring milk into the sink with the dirty dishes.

Grabbing a vitamin when you meant to take aspirin—and then wondering why your headache isn't going away.

Repeatedly pressing the off button on the microwave only to discover when the cake is burned to a crisp that you put it in the regular oven.

Putting the car in drive when you wanted to back down the driveway. Oops!

Grabbing a box of cat food instead of your box of morning cereal and not realizing it until you've already added milk.

Bending over to tie your shoes and then remembering they have Velcro.

Popping a handful of nuts into your mouth without realizing you haven't put in your dentures.

Knitting a pink scarf for a grandchild and wondering why the boy doesn't seem to like it.

Tossing out old photos and discovering you didn't save the negatives.

Judging others and then realizing you do something just as irritating or worse.

Taking a sip from your glass and then remembering you filled it with soapy water to pour on a stain in the carpet.

Hurrying out the door barefooted to get something and inadvertently locking yourself out—during a snowstorm.

Rushing off to a meeting so you won't be late, only to discover you're an hour early due to daylight savings time.

Serving ground, dried garlic when you meant to put out sugar.

Asking God to send someone to help you and then forgetting you prayed so you go ahead and try to do it yourself.

Hanging your mate's clothes on the rack in the car before you leave on vacation and not remembering for two hours that you didn't add your own.

Chasing a two-year-old grandchild while you're wearing heels so you end up at the hospital with a broken ankle.

Swallowing a time-release niacin pill when you meant to take a multivita-min tablet so you're flushed all over and your skin itches for an hour.

Forgetting while in the middle of a staircase whether you're going up or down.

Standing at the ATM and discovering you can't remember your pin number.

Handing your medical prescription to the ticket-taker at the movie theater.

Brushing your teeth with antibiotic cream.

Confusing your hearing aid on the kitchen counter with a piece of caramel from the dish beside it.

Saying yes to a slice of pecan pie and then, after eating it, remembering you're allergic to nuts.

Worrying that someday you might put the alarm clock on the back porch and wind up the cat.

Inviting your family over for a game of angiograms when you meant to say anagrams.

Setting a pot of coffee to brew but forgetting to add the water.

Pouring your soft drink into a bowl instead of a glass because you're not paying attention.

Trying to unlock the front door of your neighbor's house with your house key.

Plugging the wrong wire into the computer and wondering why it doesn't work.

Slipping the handset from your home phone into your pocket and then trying to make a phone call from the grocery store.

Running upstairs to your bedroom to change into casual clothes and getting into your pajamas instead.

Leaving the TV remote in the pantry when you get up to get a snack, looking all over for it with no success, and finding it the next day when getting ready for breakfast.

Going shopping without your list, buying everything you thought was on your list, and getting home and realizing you already have half of the stuff so now you're over your food budget.

Dropping off the black bag with garden clippings at the local charity and pitching the black bag with used clothing into the yard debris recycle bin.

Leaving the house with plans to fill your car's near-empty gas tank and then running out of gas because you forgot about it.

Putting eggs on to boil and then running an errand without turning the stove off.

Showing up for a touch football game with a baseball.

Accidentally saying "Congratulations!" when someone calls with news of a death in the family.

Going to the wrong gate at the airport and then wondering why it's taking so long for your boarding call.

Calling the locksmith to make a new house key because you locked yourself out, only to remember after he arrives that you have a spare key on a chain around your neck.

Putting your grandbaby down for a nap and then falling asleep yourself.

Donning your mate's prescription glasses by mistake and then complaining about your sudden vision problems.

Insisting you don't need a list when going to the store for two things and then having to call because you only remember one of the items.

Detailing your car because you forgot that last night's weather forecast called for rain.

Testing the smoke alarm by toasting bread on the highest setting.

Sending in a credit-card payment when your balance is zero.

Trying to send an email using a website address and then wondering why it isn't working.

Handing a 20-dollar bill to a beggar and asking for change.

Lathering your face with antifungal cream instead of shaving cream.

Going to a local charity and dropping off your mate's bag of newly purchased clothing instead of the bag of used clothing.

Trying to bake a noodle casserole in an oven set on broil.

Phoning your sister and calling her by the wrong name.

Planning to take mental acuity herbs to improve memory but forgetting to do so.

Heading to the local coffee shop to meet friends and then forgetting which one you were going to.

Trying to use a birthday card to prove your age because you've misplaced your driver's license.

Heading for the bathroom in the middle of the night but turning the wrong way when you get out of bed.

Asking your friend to monitor your house and water your plants while you're on vacation and then giving him the wrong key.

Paying a bill using the checkbook you found in a drawer, not realizing that you closed that bank account.

Trying to withdraw money from an ATM with an expired bank card.

Hiding your pin numbers and passwords for bank accounts and secure websites but not remembering where you put them when you need them.

Calling a friend and singing happy birthday and then being embarrassed when he reminds you that it's your birthday, not his.

Frosting a home-baked cake with sour cream instead of whipped cream.

Dropping the mail you just got from your post office box into the mail slot and taking home the ones you took to mail.

Accidentally using an orange instead of a lemon in a recipe.

Putting dirty clothes into the dryer instead of the washer.

Dropping off clean clothes at the dry cleaners.

Mistaking the row and seat number of your flight for the terminal and gate number and then missing your plane.

Going north when you intended to go south, and then turning left when you meant to turn right.

Trying to pay for your restaurant meal with your driver's license instead of your credit card.

Handing the flight clerk your boarding pass for a flight you took the previous year.

Opening your windows at night for fresh air and then turning on the heat in the morning without closing the windows and wondering why you're still cold.

Fertilizing the lawn before pulling the weeds.

Getting halfway through punching in a phone number and forgetting the rest of the number.

Mailing a card to a friend and then remembering you left off the street name because you wanted to double-check the spelling.

Trying to call your mom but automatically punching in the phone number of your best friend…and then having to come up with a good excuse for calling when she answers the phone.

Using foreign coins when shopping.

Putting on raspberry lip balm and then, three hours later, glancing in a mirror and realizing your lips aren't quite as wide as you thought.

Calling a podiatrist to make an appointment for a physical.

Attempting to wipe the inside of the freezer with a sponge and then spending half an hour trying to get the sponge particles off because it stuck to the surface.

Introducing your elderly musician friend by saying he's a museum.

Taking a city bus to the mall and then looking all over for your car when you're ready to leave.

Leaving home without your house keys and ID.

Putting the TV remote in the dishwasher when you're cleaning up after a televised football game.

Putting the groceries away, you suddenly realize you forgot to grab the items you put on the shopping cart's bottom shelf.

Walking across an intersection while texting and running into a parked car.

Putting hot sauce on a slice of cheesecake because you were too busy talking to paying attention.

Steaming vegetables but forgetting to put water in the steamer pot.

Getting upset when you arrive to pick up a pizza and the guy lost your phone order. On your way home, you realize you called a different pizza parlor.

Turning on the heater in the middle of summer when you meant to turn on the air conditioning.

Seasoning your hot dog with hot salsa when you meant to reach for the catsup.

Putting on your wristwatch facedown and then wondering why you can't get the band to snap closed.

Reheating the leftover dog food when you meant to reheat leftover beef stew.

Forgetting your blow-up mattress when you go tent camping.

Inserting your gas card into the ATM and getting upset when it won't let you withdraw cash.

Punching in the long-memorized telephone number of your retired friend and then being surprised when a receptionist answers.

Buttering your toast with the bacon grease you set aside in an old margarine tub.

Jumping into a hot tub before its been heated.

Backing into the garage door because you forgot to push the button on the automatic garage door opener.

Pouring birdseed into your cereal bowl and putting cereal into the bird feeder.

Forgetting to add the right amount of water to the cake mix and wondering why it didn't turn out.

Seasoning your casserole with a table-spoon of paprika when the recipe calls for a half teaspoon.

Pulling the car into the garage, you hit the button to close the door. Hearing a soft thud, you discover the door is now resting on the rear bumper.

Hearing the doorbell ring, getting up to answer it, and then realizing the doorbell was on the TV show you were watching.

Inviting your wife on a dinner date and, when she comes in all ready to go, asking, "So, what's for dinner?"

Not screwing the top on the saltshaker tightly enough so half a salt shaker's worth of salt gets poured into a recipe that only calls for a dash.

Pulling on jeans and a nightshirt and going to the mall when you meant to pull on jeans and a sweatshirt.

Grabbing a shoe brush to groom your hair.

Telling your spouse you've taken up weight lifting and then showing her by standing up from the sofa, sitting back down, and standing up again while watching TV.

Clipping the garage door opener instead of your cell phone to your belt.

Making a New Year's resolution for the year that just passed.

Putting a DVD into the CD player and becoming frustrated when it won't play.

Saying "very good" to something you couldn't really hear because you didn't want to say one more time, "What did you say?" and discovering the person just announced he was fired from his job.

Fibbing about your age and getting caught when the person asks what year you were born and you can't think fast enough to come up with the right year.

Decorating for Christmas and then realizing the next holiday is Thanksgiving.

Telling your favorite story over and over and suddenly forgetting the ending.

After struggling to make the can opener work, you discover the can of peaches has a pull-tab top.

Calling a plumber to fix a faulty television set.

Polishing your furniture with liquid soap.

Forgetting to fill up your water bottle before going on a long hike.

Stirring coffee beans instead of chocolate chips into the cookie dough.

Pouring coffee into your guests' water glasses and water into their coffee cups.

Raising a decorative flag instead of the American flag on the Fourth of July.

Standing in line to buy a movie ticket and realizing you were in the wrong line and just bought a ticket for a movie you don't want to see.

Aiming your car remote at the garage door and getting annoyed because it won't open.

Going to a special viewpoint to take great photos only to discover you forgot your camera.

Putting dishwashing soap in your clothes washing machine and clothes detergent in your dishwasher.

Dressing for bed and then driving to the store for a last-minute purchase... and wondering why people keep staring at you.

Changing from pants into a skirt and forgetting to change the type of stockings too.

Putting on your T-shirt backward and then wondering why it feels tight around your neck.

Taking your daily multiple vitamin several times a day because you can't remember if you took one already.

Swallowing an aspirin for a headache... and then one for a backache...followed by one for a stiff neck...and another for shoulder pain—all within two hours.

Forgetting the name of the bride and groom when you greet them in the wedding receiving line.

Pouring yourself a glass of apple cider vinegar instead of apple cider.

Serving cherry tomato shortcake instead of strawberry shortcake.

Forgetting your daughter-in-law's name, especially on her birthday.

Putting your money into a pants pocket, forgetting it has a hole in it.

Signing a document with your previous name when you've remarried.

Putting your pullover shirt on inside out and going shopping, and then having lunch with some friends who point out your mistake.

Asking your neighbor to feed your dog while you're on vacation only to discover you forgot to buy dog food.

Ordering a pair of sandals online and then finding out you have an identical pair on your shoe shelf.

Pouring BBQ sauce instead of chocolate sauce on ice cream and not realizing something is wrong until you see the odd look on the faces of your guests.

Leaving a box of crackers in the passenger seat of your car in a campground parking lot and discovering the next day that a bear thought they were delicious. After a $1500 new door, you're ready to continue your vacation.

Drinking Sleepytime tea for breakfast and wondering why you're so tired.

Planting sunflower seeds and when they sprout pulling them because you think they're weeds.

Sending everyone you know your change of address announcement but highlighting your previous address instead of your new one.

Waking up, dressing for the day, going outside to pick up the morning paper, and discovering it's still the middle of the night.

Eating garlic the night you promised to take your wife dancing.

Preparing a delicious chicken casserole but forgetting to add the chicken.

Offering to drive a friend to the doctor's office and then realizing your driver's license just expired.

Depositing your to-do list in the ATM slot instead of a check.

Putting your tithing check into the basket at church and forgetting to transfer the money into your bank account.

Inviting your friends over for a baked chicken dinner and, after they arrive, discovering you neglected to turn on the oven.

Baking a special pie for a neighbor who moved out the week before.

Dropping an envelope into the mailbox without putting a stamp on it first.

Getting home from a party and realizing you grabbed someone else's coat.

Hustling out the door for an appointment and not noticing till you arrive at your destination that you forgot to take off your slippers and put on your good shoes.

Sending your best friend a birthday gift six months after her actual birthday.

Choosing a password hint you won't forget, and then wondering what it refers to when it pops up on your computer screen.

Shutting off the water main when you leave on vacation, forgetting that you asked your friend to water your house-plants.

Telling your friend about a wonder-ful bumper sticker you saw on your way to church. "It was something about God…" and that's all you can remember.

# More Great Harvest House Books by Karen O'Connor

*365 Reasons Why Gettin' Old Ain't So Bad*

*Addicted to Shopping and Other Issues
Women Have with Money*

*Gettin' Old Ain't for Wimps*

*Gettin' Old Ain't for Wimps! Gift Edition*

*Grandkids Say the Cutest Things*

*Grandma, You Rock!*

*It's Taken Years to Get This Old*

*The Golden Years Ain't for Wimps*

*The Upside of Downsizing*

# Gettin' Old Ain't for Wimps

## Forging Ahead

**B**ursting with wit and wisdom, these lighthearted, real-life stories, insightful Scriptures, and heartfelt prayers will make you chuckle and confess "That sounds just like me!" Popular speaker and author Karen O'Connor invites you to celebrate the joys and misadventures of getting older. Have you noticed that...

- when you can't find your glasses, they're usually on your head?
- the delightful honesty of youth sometimes bites?
- love still makes your heart skip a beat...or two...or three?
- every morning you breathe a prayer of thanks for another day?
- a good sense of humor makes life so much easier?

Are you ready to trade in your wimp status for a more courageous existence? Or are you still wondering what lies ahead? *Gettin' Old Ain't for Wimps* hilariously affirms that life will always be filled with wonder, promise, and adventure!

# Grandkids Say the Cutest Things

## Words to Warm Your Heart

Grandkids are amazing! Gathering a charming collection of their quotes and antics, humorist and bestselling author Karen O'Connor hopes they'll brighten your day. These vignettes celebrate the candid comments and honest observations the young make about life, God, grandparents, and more.

You'll smile, chuckle, and even laugh out loud as you read these entertaining bits that are sure to remind you of the many cute things your grandkids have shared.

# The Upside of Downsizing

## Streamlining Your Life

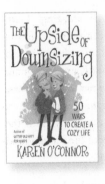

**R**eady to tackle the clutter? Wondering what to do with the extra space since the kids have moved out? Bestselling author Karen O'Connor offers encouragement and suggestions for upsizing your happiness and downsizing stress. Each short chapter includes inspiring quotes, biblical wisdom, and practical advice to help you...

- get the most out of this new life phase
- simplify and winnow responsibilities and possessions
- rediscover the joys of life without children and teens

Now is a great time to develop your interests and create a vibrant, energetic lifestyle.

To read sample chapters from Karen O'Connor's books
or to discover more great reads, go to our website:

**www.HarvestHousePublishers.com**